Thank you for sharing.

salmonpoetry

Diverse Voices from Ireland and the World

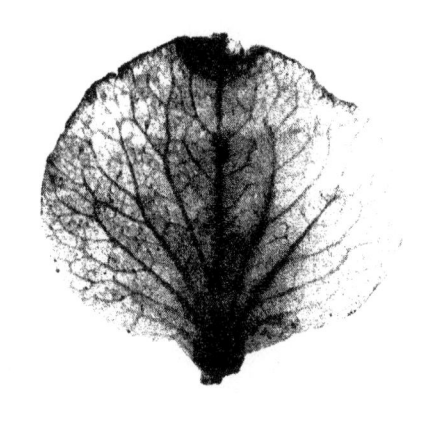

Lessons in Kindness
Dani Gill

Published in 2023 by
Salmon Poetry
Cliffs of Moher, County Clare, Ireland
Website: www.salmonpoetry.com
Email: info@salmonpoetry.com

Copyright © Dani Gill, 2023

ISBN 978-1-915022-27-1

All rights reserved. No part of this publication may be reproduced or transmitted in any form or by any means, electronic or mechanical, including photography, recording, or any information storage or retrieval system, without permission in writing from the publisher. The book is sold subject to the condition that it shall not, by way of trade or otherwise, be lent, resold or otherwise circulated without the publisher's prior consent in any form of binding or cover other than that in which it is published and without a similar condition, including this condition, being imposed on the subsequent purchaser.

Cover Image: *Fragility by Nicola Gunwhy.* Nicola Gunwhy's practice reflects on the body and place. Her work incorporates photography, text, sound, and has been exhibited internationally.

Author Photo credit: *Laura Sheeran*
Cover Design & Typesetting: *Siobhán Hutson*

Printed in Ireland by Sprint Print

Salmon Poetry gratefully acknowledges the support of
The Arts Council / An Chomhairle Ealaíon

CONTENTS

Grief

The Echo	13
Last	14
Water Angels	15
Breath	16
Silence	17
The Bird	18
Hollow	19
Collector	20
The Void	21
See You Later	22
The Gardener	23
Meaning	25
Life	26
The Jar	28

Contracts

July	31
Heart Blown Open	32
Surprise Visit	33
The Art of Peace	34
Referendum	35
The Angel Says	36
Dice	37
Cards	38
Shingles	39
I Say My Own Prayers	40

Mouthguard	41
Weather	42
Unmake	43
Nest	44
LGBT Centre Open Mic Night	45
My Heart is Sealed	46
The Uprooted Tree	47

Mirrors

In the Autumn of My Life	51
Night Walk	53
In-Breath	54
Mapping the Body	55
Border	56
The Arrow in your Heart	57
Search	58
On Stage	59
Mirror	60
Summer	61
Snow Globe	62
Perspective I	63
II	64
III	65
IV	66
Stranger on the Beach	68

Truth

For Those Who Believe in the Unseen	73
Swimmers	74
The Boat from Inis Oirr	75
Non-being	76
Names for Pain	77
Dharma Body	78
The Wave is the Water	79
Masks	80
Raise Your Spear	81
Power	82
Choose Your Weapon	83
She Who Makes Her Meaning Known	84
Truth	85
Children of Stars	86
Private Revolution	87
About the Author	89

*For my grandmother,
in your echo I stand.*

Grief

They circle me like shrouds / the women who have gone / scarves layered / around my body

The Echo

Pink and brown
mosaic squares
walking on the tiles
age six

following you up the aisle
to the tin metal box
borrowed coins
pushed through the slot

you passing us candles
long rows of flames
glowing
their red plastic circles

prayers
rising
in thin shimmers
of smoke.

Last

Under the collarbone
the pulse rapid
heaving

using the muscle to
pump pump pump
the last of the fight

the resistance I knew
you would give
your stubbornness so painful

climbing into your chariot

eyes blind to our world.

Water Angels

(for my mother)

We make water angels
rowing ourselves beneath clouds
pushing against sucked breath

the quick rise and fall of collarbones
her body coming to its end

the yellow buoy our beacon to reach
its roundness

kick our feet beneath the waves
tangle of seaweed

all things invisible
felt as a presence

the tug of current
at our ankles

I lift my head to watch you
as we swim in

making sure you are there
cutting your path

the thread of a life unravelling
our story
changing.

Breath

The pump to relieve
the swell of air
sucked into lungs

puff   puff   puffing
out

her eyes flicker to the next life

we wait
breath held

ghosts gathered to the bedside
ready to release her last

the air that will leave us winded

a scythe through the hot summer

the afternoon cut with it.

Silence

On the day after
nothing to say to the world
long hours
lying flat
on the sofa
the kitten crawling up
seeking its mother
soft on my chest
echo of my pulse
the only sound.

The Bird

Staring at the magnolia ceiling
age seven

watching shadows thrown
by cars and streetlight

having found a bird that day
dead

its soft feathers tucked around itself
a vessel

we buried it in the hedgerow
we prayed

knowing we needed to wish it well
send it to where you send the dead

when it was over
our small duty done

somewhere someone
was minding what we couldn't

the quick of a lifespan
the folded wings of an ending.

Hollow

The tiny bird rescued
in the weeks after

gathered into a towel
motherless

its silent 'o'

the mouth you remember
she made
when her words had left her

this baby mark
the shape of unheard vowels

the need to tuck in
mother it like a mother

the child you were
the child she was.

Collector

The box reveals your mysteries

a christening set
photo proofs

the objects of your life
that required protection
of tin

two feet by one foot
etched

hands go through it
at the wake

a page

the first poem I wrote
folded and kept

How did I witness you?
How did you witness me?

The Void

Your hands are in the beads
of the chain I put back together

taking linens from the hot press
for our beds
wrinkled and warm

closing the shuttered door with a
snap

disappearing into the hallway
and up the stairs

these are the sounds
that come between beads

feet on the stairway
crossing the landing

the pillow I rest my head on
when you have left the world.

See You Later

With a swing of the back gate
you are gone to do your shopping
the sunlight like the morning
of the eclipse

a stillness in the picture
an astrological glitch

it allows you to be here
leaving for town
in a summer dress

your journeys now live
in these scenes

a universe on the cusp
of what is here and
what is there
what has happened
is happening
will happen

in this moment
a pause of the record

the swing of the gate
the bottom scraping the concrete
as it always did

you there
and then not there

in the flick of a switch.

The Gardener

The underside of the roof is peeling
white wafers splinter to a hidden edge below

unidentifiable blue flower in the distance

I can feel the life in me
a pulse

my back to you
in this single room
under the stairs

steps of the nurses
an alarm
that rings

and rings

your watch idle on the locker
hands ticking
counting something
elsewhere

your breaths
 the rattle

I bring the crumpled lavender
under your nose

so that somewhere
behind your closed eyes

you might see
tall, purple spears

I've spoken memories onto the air
my voice echoing off the blue walls

all hospitals smell the same

later
peeling off my clothes
death
gone into the fibres

trying to get the odour out

in the shower
the fog of the end
now the fog of steam

and although I wanted to be there
to offer what was in me to offer

the veil of it pulled between us
left some part of me mute

you
already softened to its silence

the twitch of your eyelids when
I mentioned marigolds

how just for a second
recognition opened your milky eyes

and I looked into them searching for you
but you were already in another garden

and this hedge between us

is life, is death, is continuum.

Meaning

Maybe they carry us
and this space we are feeling

is not a void

but the wrapper
coating us

cellophane clear
pretty almost

a thin shield

the space is everywhere hugging

and yet

there is no space.

Life

(for Mervue grannies)

The grass at the races for locals with picnics
the bus into town
the jog to the bus
the memorised numbers in the black address book
the Lyons tea, the Galtee cheese
the walk to Duggan's
the open field and then the wall
that closed it in

the old peach fivers
the loveens
the ah stop
the quick flick of the extra potato
onto the edge of the still full plate
white sauce, bread sauce, a cloved onion
in the pot

tea on the range in the tin kettle
coal from the coal man
the warm smell of their crocheted cardigans
the bunions on their toes
their laughter
their shoes on the kitchen tiles
tapping out remembered tunes

the stories of their youth
their naivete
their friends, the cities they went to and
returned from
the babies lost
the children born and lost
the slanted sunset on the roof

blue wool blankets
red church candles
beads, beads in their hands
their veined, see-through skin

the vast grief
the suddenness of it

the silence after
so much bigger
than their small frames
wrapped in satin in the box

the emptiness that these
images begin to fill

the memories of

life   life   life.

The Jar

The jar is too full
memories spill over the top
too many coins

How did I collect this jar?
How do I empty you?

Contracts

"If you don't live the only life you have, you won't live some other life, you won't live any life at all."
JAMES BALDWIN

"When a woman tells the truth she is creating the possibility for more truth around her."
ADRIENNE RICH

July

I held her close
brought her poems
ballooned with hope

cast the net
caught her
and she was enough.

Heart Blown Open

When she fell in love, she said that her heart was blown open
that it took years, to pick up the pieces
a shatter, not knowing what to do next
how to love cleverly?

Her face was so soft in my hands that first summer
compass-less, I found my way around her body
and the fireworks were not instantaneous or colourful
it was just the stillness of a heart blown open

soundless mornings waking
wearing only the love she gave me.

Surprise Visit

I asked her to leave
picked up her things
like a whirlwind

it never occurred to me
to tell you not to call
or to ask her to remain
in bed with me

I handed her the brown shoes
the same ones you saw me wearing
I didn't say they were borrowed

I see her now
that morning
walking to the bus stop

how I loved her
how I hid her
omission was everything.

The Art of Peace

The challenge is to not tap out
even though the pain is suffocating
even though you can't breathe

–You are my only daughter

it was like a seed between my teeth
the princess and the pea
an undeniable something
lodged

this is what the training is for
to relax into it
to let go of 'strong'

-on the second day I dislodged it with floss

the tiny black grain
that felt like a wedge
a fleck on the enamel sink

the task is not to tap out
to find a way to breathe.

Referendum

They came home to vote
took the plane, took a boat
you drove to the end of the road
to cast your ballot-No

you said
There is a lot of sickness in the world
my 'yes' caught in my throat

celebrations in the streets

I drank to the end of restraint
promised myself more

pulled the yellow suitcase
up two flights of stairs
knocked
started fresh.

The Angel says

ISAAC: But what was I doing, tied to that altar?

ABRAHAM: You were proving your faith.

ISAAC: How?

ABRAHAM: By being the lamb that I would slaughter.

ISAAC: And why didn't you do it?

ABRAHAM: The angel said not to.

ISAAC: But who said to do it then?

ABRAHAM: God.

ISAAC: And who sent the angel?

ABRAHAM: God.

ISAAC: That's confusing.

ABRAHAM: Imagine how I feel.

Dice

In this game between us
there is a glass dice

we flick it
back and forth

sometimes it turns up
numbers

other times it looks
muddy against the cloth

the cloth is granny's lace of course
my luck rolling across the vintage white

tumbling the outcomes of our heritage

but this is not a game
and there is no dice.

Cards

On the big days
her notes

graduation
first job

how proud she was

now
cards sit in my hands
like sheets of dust

no words from her
about this new adventure.

Shingles

Thirtieth birthday
silhouette of me
walking into the sea

beneath the suit
rows of rage
dance lines along my lower back

mini eruptions
distress signals from nerves
to the surface

raised heads
that will demand cotton
and bed rest

three months later
the fogged mirror
reveals

pin pricks   each bruised dot   a lesson in kindness

how to soften in a world that
wants us to harden
how to refuse the barrier
of a tougher skin.

I say my own prayers

The lamb sucked on my finger
right before I shocked the skull
took it from its mother, the world, the metal pen

it trusted me

eyes innocent when I clamped the instrument
to its temples
resenting my power

how could they, seeing children
rape, beat and murder, a human face?
Human eyes?

I couldn't pray after that.
Not to them, not with them.
I learned to say my own prayers.

Mouthguard

Two polymer pieces
to stop the crunch
of dreams

the pressure of molar
on molar

clenching on each other
like fighters in a grip

bone to bone
root to root

ten euros and an Elvery's bag
for the thing to stop
the tension of sleep

shields for grief.

Weather

Winding roads become our July
descent into valleys

your stomach doing flips

conversations over walls with
donkeys

looking points past cliffs

lands' end

somewhere in the Atlantic
the next wind comes

knowing what is in store for us

bringing the weather.

Unmake

I've gone back to the place
with the slate

climbed over the fence
across the rocks

a rewind version of our day

tide is higher
the island more lonely

I'm sure it didn't miss this shingle
waylaid by the wall

it was after all
why you claimed it

I must try to unmake it
the journey we made

wind it back like an old cassette tape
pull the day across spools
until it's a jumble

confuse the ribbons until
the memory breaks.

Nest

I have tried to make a nest
from your daughter's hair
   ribbons over my beak

      the strands she granted me
          til you made her bald

            now only skin where gold was

my wing dissolves
into your morning tea
black tip melted
in the heat of the cup
you bring to your lips

disappearing
     is my last magic trick

LGBTQ Centre Open Mic Night

1.

*I used to hate gay people
I thought they were wrong
but then I thought of Jesus
– love one another
and I dug down inside of myself
as a Christian
and learned
to accept them.*

2.

When the missionaries first came
to our village, they raped us
then gave us the bible
this is how my faith started
I was beaten every day
by the same group of men
they said if I didn't
leave I would be murdered
I moved here with nothing
I learned to live in a new country
to be who I am without danger.

My Heart is Sealed

I knew this was different
I thought I had mourned
but no

this cloak sits across my shoulders
no tears will shift it

it was an ambush
my heart was sealed
but you got into it

this time I heard
the gates swing proper

now my heart is sealed
but with you in it.

The Uprooted Tree

Even the heaviest of things can be uprooted

its branches are a child's arms reaching out

and above deadened leaves

that identify the species

new growth   small green buds   destined for other things.

Mirrors

You are the object of your searching.

In the Autumn of my Life

It is the autumn of my life and I cross the field, wrapped in salmon pink. I walk the grass to meet you. In the spring of my life, you bore no grudges, and I had no reason to keep you from harm, only go where you were going, holding your hand.

It is the autumn of my life and I walk the field to meet you in your salmon pink. The day is blue and people have forgotten us. There are no graves or markers, everything has been. We meet in this landscape cut out for us by whatever destiny.

It is the winter of my life and I cry for you, I cry the tears I should have shed sooner. I wish you had seen what I cannot tell you. In this place it is easy to see the pain I gave you. The burdens that I carry buckle my shoulders, there is nowhere to surrender them.

It is the winter of my life and I sit on this rock. I sit here and think of the time you nearly drowned and how I would not be here if you had. I see your hands catching the reeds, and the water rushing around you. I can feel everything now, from all directions, through every skin.

It is the springtime of my life and I bear you. I deliver you into the summer, not knowing what your life will be. I continue and tend to what was there before, sometimes you do not know how to nurture a seed.

It is the springtime of my life, and I can see you. I walk with my plaits to the field and bad things happen to me. There are things you can never undo. When they ask you, you do not follow them, and I put this stone in my pocket to carry with me.

It is the springtime of my life and I cannot keep up. I think of my mother, and wish I were young again, making butter, sleeping soundly, hearing nothing.

It is the winter of your life and I help you from your chair. I comb your hair. You think that everything is forgotten but it's not, it's buried in me.

It is the winter of my life and I think of plaiting your hair, that I did not do this when you were a child, that you might hate me.

It is the winter of your life and I wonder what your masses are for, what intentions are in your rosary. At home I stay warm under my wool blankets, and I know I am a sinner.

It is the winter of my life and I want to hold you. I want to deliver you from these seasons that have been so hard.

It is the winter of your life and I know that soon I will see you, crossing the field, in your salmon pink, coming to meet me.

Night Walk

For now, it is enough
to sleep and wake up
I've grown a beard with
a silver streak

at night I walk and
imagine what I would say
if I saw someone
waiting to jump

I prepare the words
the hooks to keep them
draw to mind
reason

some nights at 3am
I pass the same drunk
stumbling home
muttering to himself

still
no-one on the rocks

I prepare the words anyway
go over them internally
loop them in my head
until I realise

the person jumping
is me.

In-Breath

The winter you went every morning
making movements toward the other side
the ritual of cold shock

waking from bad dreams
to the darkness

accepting the surrender of your dive in
resurfacing on the further rockface
released back to your sadness

there are small kindnesses in her abyss

if you go with her and ask her to move
what you cannot yet give up
a face, a name, a warm body in the dark

the tightness in your lungs
the shadows on your heart.

Mapping the Body

How much flick of the wrist
to move the ball from the waist
to the outstretched palm?

The outstretched hand that
cannot move to compensate

if it sails past an inch, a foot
you must begin again

bend and pick up
the stitched sack

re-position the arm
reach your fingers out
like someone might give you something

then place your interest in the other hand

map the distance in your mind
travel the space of your body

it floats above you
like a bird clearing a mountain
comes to rest
in the open circle of your palm.

Border

On the edge of the county
between your world and mine
I stand at a magazine rack
sandwich in one hand
stop -gapping from a wedding

chill of winter pushes
through the gap under the door
the headlines read
personal disaster
no bond solid
all possibilities of demise open

our paused love affair runs parallel
safe and un-lived
plastic lid on the tea

the promises of the staff
that they will
'see us again'

but they won't see us again
I know they won't.

The Arrow in Your Heart

It was a splinter
a speck
the small seed you picked from me

alone on the rocks
until your interruption of greeting

after that moment
both becoming less solitary

reaching out through texts
climbing steep hills in our cars
trusting safety

and now the splinter in my heart
is the arrow in yours

the sore pinch that made you
retrieve your keys

the spear that extends distance
under our skin and in our city

the wood wedge splitting a heart
re-naming destiny.

Search

Looking for you
until there is no you

only me
on this beach

playing the music I played
on my mountain

when I was both
lonely and powerful

settled in against the ruins

my cottage like a night light
behind me

in the blue grey of this evening
there is always a landscape
framing me

I learn to live in it

not look for other figures
entering or leaving.

On Stage

Up there they will love you
but not for who you are
under the lights

when you step off
who are you then?
who loves you?

In the wings
in the shadow of yourself

who?

Mirror

Half a face
streetlight
the neighbours window
reflects an obscured you

blur
your reflection
a half-moon

above your head
the real moon

a full white orb
against the dark.

Summer

The only moment we have
is this one

the dark green of the sea
beyond the edges of our shoes

our arms hugging us from
the breeze

the white of your cardigan
against my cheek

it is the first moment
it is the only moment.

Snow Globe

Our memories are summer
in a snow globe

the textures of soft hair
and Aran jumpers

I've gathered you to me
your face

it becomes the snowman

I am the rising sunlight
I am your ending.

Perspective (I)

From the scar of you
the canvas of the world stretches further

I zoom out of our counties and see continents

the lens of the drone tells me
that from ground level
small pebbles look like mountains

and from above
they become an off-white nothing

you shrink from my life
like the objects through this lens

centre and large
and then

just   a   dot.

Perspective (II)

Chasing the final hour of daylight
slipping over beach pebbles

to capture the way small puddles
become a golden double of the sun

the angle and their blackness
at that moment
a mirror for the sky

choosing to pour the last of
its power into a scatter of rock pools

they become
briefly luminous

holding clouds like mountains
in their flat dish

cupping expanse in the way
that we try to hold
our biggest wonders

until night sweeps them away.

Perspective (III)

Above the pebbles
is the golden light of sun

succeeding for twenty minutes
in a rainy day

it's the haze of a moment from
beneath our shins and knees

a ground shot of sudden magic.

Perspective (IV)

I am trying to see the world as a marble
a top and bottom
curved edges keeping everything in

the grasses and pebbles spill outside
the camera lens
messy and honest

I am talking about perspective
from your horizon to mine
where stars align and grant us
good days, luck, kind lovers

on the flip side of the circular world
the shadow of the sun chases
to the edges
of your darkness

Where am I?
Where are you?

I've found myself chasing the sunset
tapping the steering wheel impatiently
at the red lights
following twilight to the pier

scrambling across rocks and seaweed
realising that I am wearing the wrong footwear

the sudden memory of
ribcage colliding
with the flat slab
in Spiddal

my fingers reaching for the gimble
relieved to find the lens intact

the invisible bruise on my hip bone
in the days after
noticed after swimming
towelling off

the hurt of it speaking to me
reminding me that in these days of being solitary
only I will notice the damage
on my body
covered by jeans
holding itself secret

this time I don't slip
but manage to plant the camera
on the wet sand at the edge of the village

watching the purple and pink streaks
disappearing toward Aran

suddenly aware that I have
once again

come to the edge of something.

Stranger on the Beach

Bastille Day. Fireworks that mark
your exit from the emergency department
missing what you were carrying

crowds admiring red and blue
when all you can think is
–pink or blue?

You've joined a Facebook group
for women who have had
three or more
it is a specific grief
you say
the number

failed attempts to remember
who you were before

it is the quiet time of distance
and avoidance of strangers
but we have closed the gap
to staggered concrete seats
and now I know everything

when you leave
brown jacket disappearing

I wish for what they spoke of in
farmyards when we were children
–the stopping of the blood
passed from seventh son to seventh son
whispered down the phone
to a bleeding calf as the farmer cupped its ear

What incantation is there now
to share with each other?

To seal what must be sealed?
Keep it in?

Harness the love
deliver the missing.

Truth

"The moon is clear because you are clear."

DAMARA BERGER

For Those Who Believe in the Unseen

In the body there are answers
above the body there are answers
in the sky above the bay

if you pull the stillness of it to you
like a blanket
it will fill the frame

it is the rock you've noticed
the water bird behind the rock
the rock mirroring the rock
across the bay

it's the strong arm of the swimmer
slicing the water
the wetsuit breaking the surface

it is you
it is them
it is everything.

Swimmers

In the brace of the wave
we are forgotten

what was in our marrow

tossed seaweed bracelets
across our wrists

above the waterline

disappearing and re-emerging
dressed like trees of the sea

what the storm has brought
washes over us

we emerge

displaced
into a new reality.

The Boat from Inis Oirr

The moment when the grey of the sky
becomes the grey of the sea

crests rising and falling
lose their height

a limitless wall of water

until the wave is the sky
the sky is the water

we are the grey
travelling within.

Nonbeing

Somehow in this gap
there is the possibility of
not being

it is possible to fall through
cracks and keep falling

to be here in this space
is to also be nowhere

to be still
is to be falling.

Names for Pain

The colours of it
the cream of the ward
powder blue of the blankets
navy column that sits on the spine
in child's pose after the waiting is over
and the curtain falls

grey water
the centre of the pond
a ripple
watching it disperse
until there is no memory
of centre

lungs pumping
the muffle
and surrender
of sound
and then
enough

green woods
the twisted stumps that learn to lean
into each other
find space
become
dangerously immovable

the pain you say you don't have
the ache of it that sits
as disinterested as the solo magpie
outside your window
each talon gripping a grey tile
waiting for a reason to move.

Dharma Body

We reach for an edge
within ourselves
discover the soft liquid
of our core

how molten it is
the lava and mud
the honey and glue

the spike and the
softness that swallows
the blade

the possibility of more
the possibility of us
being
the more.

The Wave is the Water

Swimming at sunset
golden salt discs on the surface
find their place in the stained glass
of this painting
sulphur, laughter
people taking the plunge

the bottom of something
you can't feel
but know is there
underneath the body
clinging to shells and stones

the going is the return
the wave is the water.

Masks

When I pull this mask off
and leave it on the floor
next to the candles and feathers
it is a surprise to me too

I don't know what others I will remove

they fall from me like skins

lighter
without my armour

I move into the day
irises greener

always leaving
always arriving.

Raise Your Spear

Last week in Dublin
they called my friend a faggot
threw eggs from a passing car
this is not the country we think we live in

the first time I get a funny look
putting my arm around my girlfriend
in a bar

I remember that in another country
I could get stoned for this

then the judgement seems
like a small hate

the lump in my throat
preparing to say it
stepping out of a box I didn't make

the violence of freedom
the price we pay.

Power

You can think of twenty ways
to make something
but you can also think of twenty ways
to set someone on fire.

We drive ourselves crazy
with our greatness
ignorant of
our potential to destroy.

Choose Your Weapon

An eruption of rainbow flares
police on horseback
patrol the streets in pairs

on the other side of the archway
we go away from the water

a safer place
elevated

we must tip black water
from an aqueduct
down a drain
to save the city

a girl shows me the method
I learn to do it my own way.

She Who Makes her Meaning Clear

(after Gamba Adisa)

Under the full moon in Aries
I give up
people who don't support me
people who project on me
ideas I've had about life
ideas I have about love
loneliness.

Truth

The feather falling from the sky
on the day you need a sign
tells you what you already know

nested in your chest
pulsing

like a soft white owl
silent on its branch
surrounded by darkness.

Children of Stars

From the Taurus moon
and the sun of the archer
I am cast into this shape

from your stars you are
thrown down to the potters
wheel

a small universe contained
in bones and veins

we find each other

orbiting

children of the same maker
glitter and dark matter

seen and unseen to each other

children of sun
children of stars.

Private Revolution

I have gathered up everything that I love

without name or texture

real and imagined lovers

the words they've said

their breath

it is god

it is the light on the ocean.

Acknowledgements

Thank you Jessie Lendennie and Siobhan Hutson for your help and support, I am very proud to be a Salmon poet.

Thank you to the first readers of this work for your encouragement and feedback. Thank you to the many people I've met on this journey, who have shown me kindness in small ways and big. I am lucky and my heart is full. And to Alfie of course, you are the best.

DANI GILL is a curator, producer, writer, and educator, based in the west of Ireland. Dani served as Director of Cúirt International Festival of Literature (2010-2016), Ennis Book Club Festival (2020-2022) and has held production and creative roles in theatre and film. As an Audience Development Officer for LIVE Network, Dani works with venues and arts offices nationwide to deliver bespoke literary programmes. She holds a Diploma in Community Development and Youth Work and is motivated by projects that seek to engage, inspire and reflect community. A love of landscape and cross-artform collaboration led her to found The Lighthouse Project in 2020: site specific responses to lighthouses around Ireland. She is the Performing Arts Curator for the Bealtaine Festival and is Co-Director of Match in The Dark with Brendan MacEvilly. Her debut collection *After Love* (Salmon, 2017) was made into a dance/theatre production and premiered at the Galway International Arts Festival in 2021. A short film of the same name featured in Irish and international film festivals in 2021 and 2022.

@theedanimagic (Instagram and Twitter)

Connect with Dani

Photo credit: Laura Sheeran

salmonpoetry

Cliffs of Moher, County Clare, Ireland

"Publishing the finest Irish and international literature."
Michael D. Higgins, President of Ireland